Antlers Adorne

In the quiet of the dawn,
Antlers gleam, the world reborn.
Frosty whispers greet the day,
As winter leads us on our way.

Gathered 'round, we share our cheer,
Songs and laughter fill the sphere.
With each note, our spirits soar,
In this frost-kissed, festive lore.

In the Realm of Icy Majesty

Skates glide on ice with joyful cheer,
Children laugh, their voices clear.
In the kingdom where snowflakes twirl,
Bright lights dance and twinkle, unfurl.

Hot cocoa warms the chilly night,
While stars above shine crisp and bright.
Laughter echoes, spirits soar,
In this realm, we all explore.

Original title:
Snowlit Stags

Copyright © 2024 Swan Charm
All rights reserved.

Author: Olivia Oja
ISBN HARDBACK: 978-9908-52-758-1
ISBN PAPERBACK: 978-9908-52-759-8
ISBN EBOOK: 978-9908-52-760-4

Enchanted Whispers of the North

In the glow of lantern light,
Snowflakes dance, a pure delight.
Voices merry, laughter flows,
As the chill of winter glows.

Fires crackle, warmth in hearts,
Sharing tales where magic starts.
Stars above, like diamonds bright,
Guide us through the frosty night.

Timeless Grace in a Winter's Dream

Beneath the boughs of evergreen,
Joyful spirits can be seen.
Whispers of the past reside,
In the snow, where memories hide.

Children play with purest glee,
Building castles, wild and free.
Hot cocoa, and warm embraces,
Fill the air with joyful traces.

Winter's Gentle Majesty

Upon the hills, the soft snow lays,
Veils of white in sunlight's rays.
Nature's canvas, vast and wide,
Exudes a charm, we cannot hide.

With every breath, the crisp air sings,
Of holiday joy and wondrous things.
Frosty breath and bundled attire,
Ignite the heart, like winter's fire.

Veiled in a Shroud of White

Blankets of snow cover the ground,
Whispers of joy echo all around.
Tinsel sparkles on evergreen trees,
Happiness carried on a crisp breeze.

Candles flicker in windows aglow,
Frosted pathways where children go.
A world transformed, pure and bright,
Veiled in a shroud of snowy white.

The Quiet Majesty of Winter's Bequest

Gentle snowflakes fall from above,
Nature's silence, a gift of love.
Frost-kissed branches, a sight so rare,
In winter's majesty, we find care.

Wreaths adorn doors, a festive sight,
Families gather, hearts filled with light.
In this quiet, we find the best,
Embracing warmth, winter's bequest.

Frostfire in the Twilight

Dusk falls softly with a golden hue,
Fires crackle, casting shadows anew.
The air is crisp, the mood so bright,
  Frostfire dances in the twilight.

Jolly songs drift on the breeze,
Joyful moments bring hearts at ease.
In this glow, warmth fights the cold,
  Festivities spark, and stories unfold.

Kingdom of the Winter Spirits

In the heart of the glimmering night,
The spirits of winter take elegant flight.
With laughter like bells, they dance through the trees,
Their whispers spread joy on the crisp, frosty breeze.

Snowflakes like diamonds twirl in the air,
Each one a promise, a wish to share.
The moonlight paints shadows, a magical sight,
In the kingdom of spirits, all hearts feel so light.

Frost Enchanted Woodland Realms

Through woods where the frost weaves a silvery lace,
The trees hold their breath in this delicate space.
Tiny creatures prance with a flicker of cheer,
In a woodland enchanted, where joy is so near.

Icicles sparkle like stars in the eaves,
While whispers of laughter drift down from the leaves.
With every soft step, we stir up delight,
In the frost-kissed realms that beckon the night.

Serenade of the Icy Glimmers

A serenade flows from the icy glimmers,
With notes that entwine like shimmering whispers.
Under stars that twinkle, the world feels so bright,
With warmth in our hearts, we embrace the night.

Glistening pathways invite us to roam,
Where each frosted moment feels lovingly home.
The magic envelops, a blanket of peace,
In this tranquil realm, our worries release.

Glorious Silence Amidst the Frost

In the glorious stillness where snowflakes descend,
A blanket of white brings peace without end.
Each breath softly dances in winter's embrace,
As time takes a pause in this hallowed space.

The world glows with quiet, a shimmering hush,
Inviting us gently, away from the rush.
In this frozen moment, our spirits ignite,
In silence we find a collective delight.

A Reverie of Hooves and Crystal

In the glimmering light of midday,
Hooves dance on frost-kissed ground,
Laughter rings like a silver bell,
Joy and cheer in the air abound.

Twinkling lights in every corner,
Sparkling like stars in the night,
Children gather, wide-eyed wonder,
In the warmth of love's delight.

Fires crackle, their glow inviting,
Stories shared with each gentle breeze,
Mirthful hearts, their spirits soaring,
As winter whispers through the trees.

A festive cheer, we raise our voices,
To celebrate the magic found,
With every step, a dream rejoices,
In this revelry, we are unbound.

Parables of the Winter Seers

Snowflakes fall in delicate dances,
Covering paths in a quilt so bright,
The world adorned in white romances,
Underneath the soft silver light.

Wisdom flows from the elder trees,
Each branch holds stories to share,
With every gust, the whispers tease,
Inviting all with tales so rare.

Around the fire, tales are woven,
Of spirits that roam in the night,
Together we find comfort chosen,
In the glow of warmth, hearts ignite.

Festive spirits fill the air,
Echoes of laughter, sweet and clear,
In this season, love is everywhere,
A tapestry of joy we hold dear.

Majestic Beasts in the Twilight

In the twilight's golden hue,
Majestic beasts dance so true.
Hoofs and paws on soft earth sound,
Magic whispers all around.

Cranes take flight in fading light,
As day turns into velvet night.
Stars awaken, twinkling bright,
Joyful hearts soar with delight.

Nature's chorus fills the air,
With laughter, love, and utmost care.
Silhouettes in joyful play,
Embrace the end of another day.

Under skies painted with dreams,
Wondrous beauty fills the streams.
Together let our spirits rise,
In this realm where magic lies.

Winter's Gentle Embrace

Snowflakes dance on winter's breeze,
Whispers soft among the trees.
Joyful laughter fills the skies,
As the snowflakes twist and fly.

Children play in purest white,
Building forts with sheer delight.
Warmth of cocoa and bright fires,
Stirring hearts and warming desires.

Candles glow in every home,
Inviting all who wish to roam.
Stories shared with smiles so wide,
In the warmth of love, we abide.

Winter's song, a sweet refrain,
Bringing joy through the windowpane.
In this time of peace and grace,
Embrace the warmth of winter's face.

Beneath the Moon's Soft Glow

Beneath the moon's soft silver glow,
Whispers of night begin to flow.
Stars twinkle like diamonds bright,
Guiding dreams within the night.

Laughter dances on the breeze,
Carried gently through the trees.
Fireflies join in playful flight,
Weaving spells of pure delight.

Underneath this velvet sky,
Friendships blossom, spirits fly.
Every heart feels light and free,
In this moment, just you and me.

Let the night wrap us in peace,
In this joy, we find release.
Together we will dream and roam,
Beneath the stars, we find our home.

Frost-Kissed Wilderness

In frost-kissed fields where silence reigns,
Nature wears her icy chains.
Glistening branches reach for light,
A spectacle of pure delight.

Creatures frolic in the snow,
In a world that seems to glow.
Whispering winds, soft and low,
Guide us where the wildflowers grow.

Every step on crunching ground,
Echoes of joy all around.
Moments shared beneath the trees,
In this wonderland, hearts feel at ease.

Joyful spirits under the sun,
Chasing memories, everyone.
In the wilderness, so divine,
We find connection, pure and fine.

The Chill of Antlered Grace

In twilight's glow, the antlers rise,
A dance of light beneath the skies.
The frosty air a joyful hymn,
As nature's charm begins to brim.

Around the fire, laughter sways,
With flickering flames, it brightly plays.
Every heart feels young and free,
In the warmth of shared glee.

The forest whispers, secrets old,
Of stories wrapped in silver and gold.
With every breath, a wish is made,
In the tranquility, joy won't fade.

As stars emerge, the world ignites,
With hopes reborn on tranquil nights.
Together we stand, a serendipitous grace,
In the chill of antlered embrace.

When the Forest Holds Its Breath

The trees stand tall, in silence deep,
As nature holds the dreams we keep.
With every rustle, a secret shared,
In the quiet, the world is spared.

The colors burst, from green to gold,
Magic weaves its stories told.
With golden leaves that dance and twirl,
Through the air, a festive whirl.

Laughter echoes, a joyous sound,
As joy and love in circles abound.
With sparkling eyes, we feel alive,
In this moment, we all thrive.

The forest hums a tender tune,
Beneath the watchful, silver moon.
In every breath, a hope entwined,
When the forest hums and love is kind.

Glistening Requiem of the Woods

With frosted boughs and glistening dew,
The woods awake, a joyful view.
Nature's splendor, in icy lace,
A festival of light in wild embrace.

The whispers of leaves, a gentle sound,
While spirits lift from hallowed ground.
In every shadow, a moment gleams,
As laughter flows, like flowing streams.

Crisp air tinged with scents divine,
A celebration, our hearts align.
In the hush, we find our place,
A glistening requiem, a sacred space.

The starlit sky invites us near,
With open hearts, we draw in cheer.
In nature's arms, we learn to sing,
Embraced by woods, as joy takes wing.

Elysium in White

A blanket soft of purest white,
Cloaks the world in magical light.
With every step, a dazzling crunch,
In playful dances, we all lunch.

The snowy branches, a frozen dream,
Reflecting joy, like a glimmering stream.
We weave our stories, hearts unite,
In the chill of a festival night.

With candle flickers, warmth abounds,
As laughter echoes in leaps and bounds.
Together we craft our winter's tale,
In this Elysium, we shall prevail.

As stars shine bright, like diamonds rare,
We share our wishes, hopes laid bare.
In the embrace of white, all fears take flight,
Elysium dances, our spirits igniting bright.

Echoes of Antlers in the Moonlight

In the glimmer of a silver night,
Antlers rise with a graceful sight.
Whispers dance on the evening breeze,
Songs of joy in the swaying trees.

Beneath the stars, laughter abounds,
Nature's pulse in the heart resounds.
Flickering lights in the shadowed glade,
Memories woven, never to fade.

Mirthful deer leap in playful cheer,
Their merry hearts, so bright and clear.
A tapestry of warmth and light,
Echoes linger in the still of night.

The Stillness of the Woodland Watchers

In the quiet woods, the watchers stand,
Guardians of joy, a whimsical band.
Leaves shimmer with a golden glow,
While secrets of the night gently flow.

Stars winking in the vast expanse,
Creatures gather for a playful dance.
Echoes of laughter fill the air,
Festive spirits everywhere.

Mushrooms bloom in their vibrant dress,
Nature's canvas, pure happiness.
A symphony of sights and sounds,
Harmony in the heart abounds.

Frosted Paths Under Celestial Canopies

Frosted paths trace a silver line,
Under the canopy where stars align.
Quiet footsteps, a soft sweet sound,
Festivity in the air all around.

Crystals glimmer like whispered dreams,
Nature's beauty, or so it seems.
Moonbeams dance on the frozen ground,
A magical world, wonder is found.

In the stillness, joy intertwines,
As every heart in delight shines.
The night whispers secrets that delight,
Frosted paths in the soft moonlight.

Enigma of the Frozen Glade

In the frozen glade, magic awaits,
Where frolicsome spirits open the gates.
Snowflakes twirl in a graceful flight,
Mysteries held in the silent night.

A gentle hush blankets the scene,
Nature's wonders, pure and serene.
Whispers of joy on the frosty air,
Echoes of laughter, banishing care.

Frosty breath in the crisp, clear space,
Every moment, we embrace with grace.
In the stillness, hearts intertwine,
A festive spirit, forever divine.

Hall of Antlers in the Icebound Canopy

In the hall of frost where stillness reigns,
Antlers glimmer like moonlit chains.
Chimes of laughter drift through the air,
Gifts of Nature, beyond compare.

Snowflakes twirl, a cheerful crowd,
Dancing soft, as if they're proud.
Under the boughs, bright spirits rise,
Reflecting joy in winter skies.

Icicles hang like crystal streamers,
Caroling winds are festive dreamers.
The world aglow, a splendid sight,
In this canopy, a pure delight.

Whispers of the Glacial Shadows

Whispers float in the frosty night,
Glacial shadows dance with light.
Frigid air carries joyful sound,
In this cold, warm hearts abound.

Twinkling stars are a festive cheer,
Greeting all with warmth so near.
Each corner of ice sparkles and shines,
Creating memories as bright designs.

Laughter mingles with the night breeze,
Bringing smiles, a sweet reprieve.
Underneath the frozen trees,
Echoes of joy are carried with ease.

Echoing the Winter's Soliloquy

In the silence, the winter sings,
Echoes soft on silver wings.
A soliloquy of chilly bliss,
Wrapped in warmth, we reminisce.

Fires crackle, casting glow,
An ambiance of joy we sow.
Crimson and gold weave and play,
Marking time in a splendid way.

Cider warms in festive hands,
Voices lift in merry bands.
In this frosted, bright embrace,
Magic lingers in every space.

A Luminescent Dance of the Quiet Realm

In the quiet realm, a dance takes flight,
Luminescent sparkles pierce the night.
Winter's grace, a gentle sway,
Holds enchanting moments at bay.

Snow drifts soft underfoot,
With each whisper, the spirits root.
Joyful hearts leap with delight,
Under the glow of lantern light.

Hand in hand, we roam the fields,
Where magic, like warmth, gently yields.
Every step, a rhythmic beat,
In this winter, our souls meet.

Gleaming Antlers in the Stillness

In the hush of frosty nights,
Gleaming antlers catch the light.
Stars twinkle in a velvet sky,
As whispers of the season sigh.

Gathered round the fireside glow,
Laughter dances, warm and slow.
Mugs of cocoa, sweet delight,
We celebrate this wondrous night.

Snowflakes fall with gentle grace,
Blanketing the earth's embrace.
Joy in every heart ignites,
In this magical, wintry night.

With friends and family so near,
Peace and love is crystal clear.
Gleaming antlers in the stillness,
A festive mood, a heartfelt thrillness.

The Dance of the Frozen Heart

Underneath the silver moon,
Hushed enchantments make us swoon.
Frozen hearts begin to sway,
In the dance of night and day.

Glittering lights on branches sway,
Magic moments lead the way.
Footsteps crunch on blankets white,
As laughter fills the frosty night.

Winds of joy, they gently spin,
Whispers of the night begin.
Wrapped in warmth, we twirl and glide,
In the festive air we bide.

Join me in this fleeting chance,
As we lose ourselves in dance.
Hearts united, never part,
Together shares the frozen heart.

In the Quiet of the Snowfall

Snowflakes drift like whispered dreams,
In soft silence, nature gleams.
Blankets of white cushion the ground,
In the quiet, joy is found.

Children's laughter fills the air,
Building snowmen everywhere.
Warmth of cocoa in our hands,
Magic lives in winter lands.

Candles flicker, shadows play,
As we gather at the end of day.
Stories shared by firelight,
Make the world feel warm and bright.

In the quiet, hearts align,
Sparkling moments feel divine.
Snowfall dances all around,
In this festive joy, we're found.

Echoes Amongst the Pines

Beneath the pines, the echoes call,
Festive spirits cheer for all.
Whispers of the wind delight,
As stars adorn the canvas night.

Fires crackle, shadows leap,
Joyful memories we will keep.
Sweets and treats line every table,
Stories shared, all friends are able.

With every twinkle, laughter rings,
In this place, the spirit sings.
Together we find magic's art,
Echoes of love fill every heart.

Underneath the starlit dome,
In the pines, we feel at home.
Celebrate with song and cheer,
Magic moments, ever near.

Elegance in Frost

Beneath the glow of twinkling lights,
Snowflakes dance on velvet nights.
Joyful laughter fills the air,
As hearts unite in seasonal care.

Icicles shimmer, a crystal show,
Every branch draped in winter's glow.
A feast awaits, where friends convene,
In a world wrapped in silvery sheen.

Candles flicker, warm and bright,
Casting shadows in the night.
With every toast and cheer around,
A magic sparkles, love is found.

The elegance of frost, a gentle muse,
Whispers of warmth in the chilly blues.
In every smile, and every glance,
We celebrate winter's blissful dance.

Whispers of the Winter Grove

In the grove where silence sings,
Winter weaves its silver strings.
Crystalline branches in soft embrace,
Nature dons her frosty lace.

Snow-draped paths beckon us near,
Whispers of joy echo clear.
Children laughing, a pure delight,
As snowflakes twirl in joyous flight.

Hot cocoa warms, as fires crackle,
Stories shared, while spirits tackle.
In this haven, joy takes its form,
As hearts gather in peaceful warm.

The winter grove, a sacred space,
With each breath, a warm embrace.
In laughter's echo and love's soft glow,
We find the magic in winter's snow.

Antlers Adorned in White

Amidst the pines, a figure strides,
Antlers crowned, where magic hides.
Whispers of snow on velvet ground,
A festive spirit all around.

Creatures gather, fur and feather,
In this realm, we share the tether.
Laughter mingles with the breeze,
As joy entwines through winter trees.

The air is crisp, with scents divine,
Gathered friends around the pine.
With every song and every cheer,
The warmth of love draws us near.

Antlers adorned in purest white,
Under stars that twinkle bright.
In every heart, a spark ignites,
Celebrating winter's joyful nights.

Shadows of the Silent Woods

In the woods where shadows play,
Winter's magic lights the day.
Deer move softly, grace on feet,
While hearts gather, the world feels sweet.

Branches heavy with frosted dreams,
Echoes of laughter spill in streams.
With every step, the hush is clear,
A symphony of joy we hear.

Candles flicker in the night,
As friends embrace the festive light.
With every story shared in trust,
In winter's beauty, we find our must.

Shadows dance in the silent woods,
A tapestry of joy and goods.
Together we weave memories bright,
In the heart of this winter night.

The Velvet Chill of Winter's Breath

A gentle whisper in the night,
The world adorned in silver light.
Laughter dances with the frost,
In winter's arms, no joy is lost.

Bright lanterns twinkle in the trees,
While joy is carried by the breeze.
Warm mugs cradle in our hands,
A moment shared, as friendship stands.

Snowflakes twirl like stars above,
We gather close, wrapped in love.
Under moonlit skies we play,
In this festive night, we sway.

The velvet chill, our hearts ignite,
In winter's grasp, pure delight.
Together we will sing and cheer,
For this is our time of the year.

Enchantment Beneath the Avalanche

Beneath the weight of glistening snow,
An adventure waits, a chance to grow.
The mountains hum a festive tune,
As day gives way to glowing moon.

With sleds and laughter, down we glide,
A winter's thrill, a joyous ride.
Magic swirls in the frigid air,
In every heart, there's love to share.

We build our dreams in castles tall,
As snowflakes drift like whispered calls.
Hands intertwined, we venture forth,
In winter's grip, we find our worth.

Enchantment flows through every breath,
A celebration of life, not death.
Together we lift our spirits high,
Underneath the vast, winter sky.

Boughs of Serenity in the Frost

Branches heavy with snowflakes cling,
Whispers of peace that winter brings.
The world drapes soft in frosted veils,
As laughter floats through snowy trails.

Beneath the boughs, we find our place,
In quiet moments, we embrace.
Candles flicker with a warm glow,
In this serene, enchanted show.

The stars awaken, shining bright,
In the canvas of the night.
Together we cherish every sight,
As joy sparkles in pure delight.

A sanctuary within the chill,
In nature's calm, we find our thrill.
With every heartbeat, we rejoice,
Together, we make the world our choice.

Where Time Stands Still in the Snow

In a realm where silence reigns,
Time slows down as joy remains.
Soft whispers float on icy air,
As peace enfolds us everywhere.

Frosted pines stand tall and proud,
Underneath the shimmering cloud.
We share our stories by the fire,
As flames flicker with pure desire.

In this moment, worries cease,
Our hearts are filled with warmth and peace.
The snowflakes dance like fleeting dreams,
In this festive land, or so it seems.

Where time stands still, our spirits soar,
With love and laughter, forevermore.
Together we weave memories bright,
In the embrace of the winter night.

Journey Through the Luminescent Woods

In the woods where light does dance,
Colors twirl in a vibrant trance.
Fireflies float on whispering breeze,
Magic lingers among the trees.

Laughter echoes beneath the leaves,
Joyful hearts, no one deceives.
Pathways shimmer, all aglow,
Wandering where the wild things grow.

Candles flicker in the night,
Guiding souls with warmth and light.
Each step glimmers, pure delight,
In this realm of wondrous sight.

As starlit skies begin to fade,
The dreams we weave will not evade.
Through the woods, our spirits soar,
Together, forever, we explore.

Beneath the Arctic Canopy

Beneath the skies of sparkling white,
We dance with joy, hearts feeling light.
Snowflakes swirl like a playful breeze,
Whispers of winter in frosted trees.

The world adorned in icy lace,
Every moment a warm embrace.
Bright lights twinkle, a festive show,
In the Arctic's embrace, we glow.

Laughter rings through the frozen air,
As merry souls spin without care.
With friends around, the warmth ignites,
Celebrating through long, starry nights.

In this wonderland tucked away,
We cherish each moment, come what may.
Beneath the canopy, spirits rise,
As dreams take flight beneath the skies.

Guardian Spirits of the Wintry Woods

In the silence of the snow-kissed night,
Ancient spirits dance in soft moonlight.
Branches whisper, secrets unfold,
Tales of guardians, brave and bold.

The snowflakes fall with gentle grace,
Enchanting beauty in this sacred space.
Together we gather, hearts entwined,
In the warmth of the stories enshrined.

Paths of silver lead us near,
Echoes of laughter, friendships dear.
Each step a promise, bright and clear,
In wintry woods, we shed all fear.

With spirits guiding us along,
In this wonderland, we all belong.
Through whispered tales and frosty nights,
Our joyous hearts reach soaring heights.

Frosted Elegance in Twilight's Glow

Twilight dances on frosted ground,
A tapestry of beauty all around.
Glistening snowflakes twirl with grace,
In the chill, we find our place.

Elegance wrapped in silver light,
Every shadow holds a sparkly bite.
Candles flicker, whispers of glee,
Gathered together, just you and me.

Hot cocoa warms our waiting hands,
Laughter mingles across snow-clad lands.
Frosted dreams take elegant flight,
In the glow of the soft, starry night.

As we cherish this wondrous view,
Frosted elegance, pure and true.
In twilight's charm, our hearts will sing,
For together, we embrace the spring.

Spirits of the Winter Realm

Whispers dance in the chilly air,
A symphony of joy everywhere.
Snowflakes tumble, twirling free,
Nature's grace in pure esprit.

Cheerful laughter fills the night,
Lanterns glow, hearts feel light.
Warming fires in a cozy glow,
Haven found in the winter snow.

Sparkling dreams in each frosty breath,
Celebrating life, defying death.
Under stars like diamonds bright,
Gathered together, we share delight.

Songs of old fill the festive air,
Magic lingers everywhere.
Toasting to the spirits near,
In winter's heart, we hold our cheer.

A Soft Step on Crystal Ground

A gentle hush falls on the earth,
Winter whispers, giving birth.
To moments sweet, soft as a sigh,
Bringing warmth as time drifts by.

Footprints twinkle like stars anew,
In the moonlight's silvery hue.
With every step, the magic sings,
Joy and wonder that winter brings.

Frosty branches, a glistening sight,
Crafting beauty in the night.
Echoes of laughter mingle and play,
In this realm where dreams weave and sway.

Sipping cocoa by the fireside,
Here in warmth, our hearts abide.
Rays of light through the crystal mist,
Moments like these, we can't resist.

Luminous Tracks in the Ether

Glimmers shimmer in the night sky,
As we watch the stars drift by.
Each sparkling light a guiding beam,
In this enigma, we dare to dream.

With every twirl, our spirits lift,
In this season, a time to gift.
The dance of shadows, bright and bold,
Whispers of warmth despite the cold.

Candles flicker in a joyful spree,
An invitation to just be free.
Voices raised in a tuneful song,
In the glow of night, we all belong.

Follow the tracks where laughter leads,
In the winter's heart, love feeds.
As we gather under starlit nights,
Creating moments, our hearts ignite.

Woven Tales of Frost and Light

In the chill, stories unfold,
Woven tales more precious than gold.
A tapestry of laughter and cheer,
Each thread a memory held near.

Frosty mornings bring a gleam,
Of whispered words and childhood dreams.
Families gather, bonds entwined,
In this season, our hearts aligned.

Under the trees with branches bare,
We share our secrets with the air.
Tales of old, both dear and bright,
Illuminate the long, cozy night.

As the embers glow deep and red,
We weave our stories, the words are spread.
With every laugh, a magic chord,
In winter's embrace, our spirits soared.

Whispers of the Winter Wood

Beneath the shimmer of gentle lights,
The wood breathes soft in winter's embrace.
Snowflakes dance as laughter ignites,
Nature's joy unfolds in this place.

Children's giggles fill the air,
Footprints trace stories in pure white.
Whispers of magic linger there,
As twinkling stars adorn the night.

Pine trees wear their frosty crowns,
While shadows play in the moon's glow.
Every heart twirls and spins around,
In this wonderland, spirits flow.

Cupped in warmth of fireside hearts,
We toast to dreams that come alive.
In winter's wood, where love imparts,
The festive spirit will always thrive.

Grace Amongst the Falling Flakes

In the hush of a frosty dawn,
Flakes cascade like whispered dreams.
Nature dons her glittering gown,
While laughter glows in silver beams.

Children twirl in joyful delight,
Creating angels, pure and bright.
With every flake, a world to share,
Grace flows softly through the air.

Hot cocoa warms the chilly hands,
As stories spark by crackling fire.
Together, we weave joyful plans,
Fulfilling every heart's desire.

In this moment, hearts convene,
Beneath the canopy of light.
In winter's grace, pure and serene,
We celebrate the night's delight.

The Silent Choreography of Hooves

In the meadow where snowflakes fall,
Gentle hooves tread a soft-hued dance.
With every step, a silence calls,
The beauty of winter's sweet romance.

Horses prance with spirited grace,
Every leap, a whisper of joy.
In their rhythm, we find our place,
Nature's beauty, no one can destroy.

The skies drape low, a silver sigh,
As frost-kissed shadows begin to play.
Beneath the canopy, hearts can fly,
Finding magic in the simplest way.

With laughter echoing through the trees,
We join the dance in fluffy white.
In this tranquil world, we find our ease,
The silent choreography ignites the night.

Silvered Echoes of the Forest

In the depths of the moonlit glade,
Silver beams dance through branches bare.
Each echo tells of memories made,
Whispers of joy ride the winter air.

The forest breathes in peaceful calm,
Wrapped in blankets of crystalline white.
Every heartbeat is a sweet psalm,
As stars twinkle with pure delight.

Fires crackle, casting golden light,
While stories linger on hopeful tongues.
Festive spirit ignites the night,
As we've gathered, old and young.

With laughter trailing through the trees,
We weave our dreams in frosty air.
In these moments, we find the keys,
To silvered echoes of love and care.

Celestial Glow Beneath the Pines

Beneath the pines, a glow so bright,
Twinkling stars in the crisp night.
Laughter mingles with frosty air,
Joy and warmth, a festive flair.

Candles flicker in the snow,
Whispers shared, voices low.
Decked in gleam, the trees inspire,
Hearts lifted, dreams transpire.

Silent night, the world aglow,
Magic dances, spirits flow.
Gathered close, friends by my side,
In this moment, we abide.

A chorus sung with sweet delight,
Echoes of love fill the night.
Beneath the pines, together we sway,
In celestial glow, we find our way.

Frosted Giants in the Glade

Tall and proud, the giants stand,
Frosted crowns across the land.
Snowflakes fall like gentle sighs,
Natures' charm in winter skies.

Children dance in joyful play,
Beneath the arms of trees so sway.
Giggles echo through the air,
A festive spirit everywhere.

Crimson berries pop with cheer,
Glistening bright, they seem so near.
With each step, the magic grows,
In the glade, where wonder flows.

Frosted giants guard our night,
While twinkling stars offer light.
In whispers shared and laughter bright,
We celebrate this pure delight.

The Starlit Dance of Solitude

In solitude beneath the stars,
A dance unfolds, a dream from afar.
Silence wraps the world so tight,
Each twirl sings of pure delight.

Steps of joy on glistening ground,
In the night, sweet peace is found.
Shadows dance in the moon's warm glow,
Where hearts listen, and spirits flow.

Twinkling lights hold secrets dear,
Every breath brings the night near.
In this hush, the world stands still,
With every beat, our hearts we fill.

The starlit path leads us to grace,
With every turn, a warm embrace.
In solitude, together we sway,
In the dance, joy finds its way.

Elegance in the Chilling Breeze

A chilling breeze with elegance flows,
As laughter rises, the magic grows.
Scarves wrapped tight, we stroll in style,
With each heartbeat, we pause awhile.

The moonlight glistens on soft white ground,
Echoes of joy in every sound.
Dancing shadows, flickering light,
In this chill, our hearts ignite.

Hot cocoa sipped by the fire's glow,
Stories spun in the evening's flow.
With cookies shared, our spirits soar,
In the chill, we find much more.

Beneath the stars, we dream anew,
In this festive air, hopes accrue.
Elegance blooms in the winter's tease,
With warmth in hearts, and love that frees.

The Golden Age of Tranquil Realms

In gardens bright with blooms in cheer,
Laughter dances in the air,
Underneath the sun's warm glare,
Joyful hearts draw ever near.

With gentle winds that softly play,
Children's voices rise like song,
Every moment feels so strong,
In this golden light of day.

Breezes carry tales of old,
Whispers shared, and dreams unfold,
Magic weaves through every thread,
In a tapestry of gold.

So let's raise a glass and cheer,
To the moments that we share,
In this golden age so rare,
Love and laughter bring us near.

Majestic Silence of the Winter Realm

Snowflakes dance on silent ground,
Moonlight glistens, pure and bright,
In this tranquil, frosty night,
Every breath is peace profound.

Stars above in velvet skies,
Whispers of the night unfold,
Stories in the snow, retold,
As the world in slumber lies.

Fires crackle, warmth ignites,
Hot cocoa steaming in our hands,
Gathered close, our hearts expand,
In the glow of winter lights.

Joy abounds in this still space,
Every laugh, a sweet embrace,
In this realm of white and freeze,
We find beauty, love, and peace.

Antlered Phantoms in a Glacial Land

Through frosty woods, the phantoms glide,
Antlers high, they roam in grace,
Veiled in mist, they leave no trace,
In a world both wild and wide.

Moonlit shadows paint the trees,
Whispers echo in the chill,
Nature's beauty, calm and still,
Carried softly on the breeze.

Gleaming frosts like diamonds shine,
Every step a fleeting dance,
In a realm of pure romance,
Where the wild and peaceful intertwine.

Let us pause to softly sigh,
In this magic that surrounds,
With phantoms where the silence bounds,
Underneath the starry sky.

In the Heart of the Crystal Kingdom

Glistening walls of ice and light,
Echo laughter, pure delight,
In this realm of crystal grace,
Magic weaves its fond embrace.

Candles flicker, shadows play,
Songs of joy fill every room,
Glorious in winter's bloom,
As we dance the night away.

Sparkling jewels, the snowflakes fall,
Chiming bells, a festive cheer,
Gathered loved ones drawing near,
In the heart, we feel it all.

Beneath the arching icy boughs,
Promises through laughter flow,
In this kingdom, love will grow,
Together here, we take our vows.

A Journey Through the Crystal Wilderness

In crystal woods where shadows glimmer,
The light dances bright, a festive shimmer.
With laughter ringing through the trees,
The magic stirs with every breeze.

Snowflakes twirl like stars above,
Whispering secrets of winter's love.
Together we wander, hand in hand,
In a wonderland, so soft, so grand.

The paths are lined with sparkling white,
As we chase dreams in pure delight.
Each step a story waiting to unfold,
In this enchanting realm of cold.

A journey where the heart takes flight,
In the embrace of the frosty night.
With every moment, joy is near,
In the crystal wilderness we hold dear.

Treading Lightly in the Frozen Dream

Through quiet glades where silence sings,
We tread lightly under silver wings.
Each breath a whisper in the air,
In this frozen dream, without a care.

The world adorned in frosty lace,
A wintry ball, a timeless grace.
With every heartbeat, warmth we find,
In the joyous chill that binds our kind.

Footprints dance on sparkling ground,
With every laugh, pure joy abounds.
A festive spirit fills the night,
As stars awaken, glowing bright.

In this realm where time stands still,
We celebrate with hearts that thrill.
A poignant journey through the gleam,
Together we weave this frozen dream.

Encounters in the Dappled Frost

Beneath the trees where frost does weave,
We meet with smiles, neither naive.
In dappled light, the laughter flows,
Among the branches, friendship grows.

The air is crisp, a joyous sound,
As we gather 'round, our spirits found.
With every tale and joyful cheer,
The magic lingers, ever near.

Snowflakes drift like whispered dreams,
Illuminating our hopeful beams.
In nature's wonder, we unite,
Creating memories, pure delight.

Encounters here, so rare and sweet,
In shimmering worlds beneath our feet.
In this festive dance, hearts align,
In dappled frost, our souls entwine.

Heartbeat of the Winter's Guardians

In echoes of the winter's breath,
We find a rhythm, defying death.
The heartbeat of guardians, strong and true,
Guides our steps in a world so new.

With every flake, a story told,
Of warmth within the bitter cold.
A festive spirit swirls alive,
In the heart of winter, hopes revive.

Beneath the moon, we spin and sway,
Entwined in joy, we dance and play.
With laughter bright as starlit skies,
In unity, our spirits rise.

Each heartbeat mirrors nature's song,
A celebration where we belong.
Together we honor this frosty land,
As guardians rise, hand in hand.

A Tapestry of Ice and Grace

Frosted branches glisten bright,
Children's laughter fills the night.
Candles flicker, warmth in air,
Magic dances everywhere.

Snowflakes twirl with joyful spin,
Whispers of a world within.
Heartfelt cheers and voices soar,
Moments cherished, evermore.

Twinkling lights on every street,
Gathered friends, a festive treat.
Songs of joy in winter's hold,
Stories shared and love retold.

From the hearth, a spirit bright,
Celebration, pure delight.
A tapestry we weave today,
In harmony, we laugh and play.

Beyond the Veil of Silent Pines

In the hush of falling snow,
Whispers travel, soft and slow.
Underneath the starlit skies,
Joyful hearts begin to rise.

Pine trees draped in silver hue,
Gatherings of spirits, true.
Feasts adorned with endless cheer,
Echoes of the season near.

Candied fruits and spiced delight,
Songs of hope throughout the night.
Hands entwined, a circle wide,
Love and laughter, side by side.

Beyond the veil, the magic stirs,
In every heart, the winter purrs.
Together, we embrace the glow,
In this moment, let us flow.

Guardians of the Unyielding Chill

Through the frozen fields we roam,
Crafting warmth that feels like home.
Candles flicker in the night,
Guardians of a love so bright.

Echoes of the past resound,
In this space, joy can be found.
Winter's breath, a gentle kiss,
In the cold, we find our bliss.

Fires crackle, stories weave,
In this magic, we believe.
Hearts entwined through all the trials,
Genuine warmth, our lasting smiles.

Silent nights, where dreams take flight,
In the stillness of the night.
Guardians raised against the chill,
Together, we embrace the thrill.

Domains of the Winter Kings

In the land of glittered white,
Winter kings hold court tonight.
Glories sung of days gone past,
Memories that ever last.

Frosted castles gleam and shine,
In this realm, our hearts align.
With every laugh, with every cheer,
We celebrate our loved ones near.

Hushed whispers of a snow-capped dawn,
In this magic, we are drawn.
Glowing embers warm the soul,
As the festive spirits roll.

With each toast, we raise our cheer,
In the radiance, hearts are clear.
Domains where joy and love are kings,
In harmony, our spirit sings.

The Ethereal Requiem in the Snowbound Grove

In the grove where whispers flow,
Snowflakes dance with a gentle glow.
Lights twinkle like stars at dusk,
Hearts entwined in a soft husk.

Laughter spills like wine so sweet,
Echoes of joy, a rhythmic beat.
Around the fire, tales are spun,
Under the blanket of the setting sun.

Carols rise on the frosty air,
Joyful spirits everywhere.
The world aglow in silvery light,
An ethereal dance in the quiet night.

Memories wrapped in the winter's embrace,
Each bond cherished, each smile a trace.
In this grove where dreams take flight,
The requiem sings of pure delight.

Moment of Solitude Under the Silent Skies

Beneath the canvas of twilight's hue,
Stars twinkle softly, a dream come true.
The world holds its breath, wrapped in peace,
In the silence, all worries cease.

A single moment, profound and still,
Whispers of nature lend their thrill.
In solitude's arms, one finds a song,
A melody sweet, where hearts belong.

Shadows dance on the silvered ground,
In this quiet, true magic is found.
Each twinkling star shares a secret wish,
As dreams awake in a midnight swish.

Through the calm, hope starts to rise,
Confirmation lives in the silent skies.
A moment cherished, a treasure near,
In the stillness, the heart draws near.

Legends of Ice-Touched Titans

In realms where the cold winds reign,
Legends whisper in frosty vein.
Titans stand with their icy gaze,
Crafting tales in the winter's haze.

Strength embodied in their stance,
In the chill, they twist and dance.
Silent power, ageless and bold,
Stories of warmth amidst the cold.

Snowflakes shimmer like shards of light,
Each one tells of a wondrous night.
Echoing laughter, a haunting sound,
In the legends of the lost, we're bound.

Through ice and snow, their spirits glide,
Eternal guardians by our side.
In this world where dreams ignite,
We celebrate the souls of night.

The Serene Call of the Glacial Heart

Within the silence, a heartbeat glows,
A call of peace where the soft wind blows.
Ice-crystal echoes, a gentle sigh,
Whispers of beauty, so high, so nigh.

The glacial heart, steady as stone,
Guides us gently, we are not alone.
In the stillness, warmth is found,
A serene calm wraps all around.

With every breath, the cold bites sweet,
Lengthened shadows, dancing feet.
In icy realms, where dreams unfold,
The heart's own story is softly told.

As twilight deepens, a soothing lore,
The glacial heart opens magic's door.
Together we gather, lost in delight,
Amidst the calm of the evening light.

Frost-Kissed Monarchs at Dusk

The crisp air glows with winter's grace,
As monarchs twirl in frosty lace.
Their laughter dances on the breeze,
A symphony beneath the trees.

With each step, a crunch, a cheer,
The world transformed, so bright, so clear.
Snowflakes twinkle, soft as dreams,
In this realm, joy brightly beams.

Glistening crowns upon their heads,
Through twilight paths where magic spreads.
They share their warmth, igniting night,
In festive wonder, pure delight.

Oh, let the memories align,
Of laughter sweet like aged red wine.
For in this moment, all feels right,
Frost-kissed monarchs share the light.

The Quietude of Nature's Sovereigns

In nature's arms, the still winds sigh,
Beneath the twinkling midnight sky.
The sovereigns of the grove unite,
In gentle dances of starlit light.

Branches swaying, shadows play,
Beneath the moon, they find their way.
Soft whispers fall like snowflakes light,
In this quietude, hearts take flight.

Gleaming eyes that hold the stars,
Echoes of joy, no sign of scars.
They revel in the tales of old,
In nature's lore, their spirits bold.

Oh, gather near, let laughter swell,
In unity, let stories tell.
For every breath, a song divine,
In quietude, we intertwine.

Radiance in the Whispering Woods

Among the trees where shadows weave,
A magic forms, a dream to believe.
Radiance glimmers in every nook,
As joy ignites with every look.

The leaves murmur with secrets shared,
In festive spirits, all unprepared.
Footfalls light on the emerald floor,
In whispering woods, we welcome more.

Colors burst like laughter free,
Nature's canvas is all we see.
Twinkling lights strung on every branch,
Invite us all to join the dance.

So let the night sing wild and clear,
In every heart, there's nothing to fear.
Together we'll tread where magic stood,
Finding our joy in the whispering wood.

Beneath a Veil of Winter's Breath

A silken veil of winter's breath,
Wraps the world in cozy rest.
Beneath the stars, where dreams alight,
We gather close, our hearts delight.

The crackling fire warms the night,
As laughter echoes, hearts take flight.
Footprints mark the snowy trail,
In our spirit, we shall not fail.

Snowflakes dance on whispers' wings,
As nature's choir softly sings.
With every flake, a tale unfolds,
In winter's grip, our joy beholds.

Together we'll weave through frosty air,
Bound by love, a bond so rare.
Beneath this veil, so soft, so bright,
We celebrate together, pure delight.

Shadows of the Woodlands' Kings

In the heart of the woodland, shadows play,
Dancing lights beside the ancient oak's sway.
Whispers of laughter on the cool night air,
Magic unfurling, weaving joy everywhere.

Underneath the starlight, dreams take flight,
Crowned in mirth, the woodland is bright.
Glimmers and twinkles, a festive parade,
As shadows come alive in a vibrant charade.

Songs of the forest, a chorus, they sing,
Celebrating life, embracing the spring.
Each footfall a rhythm, each heartbeat a cheer,
In the shadows of kings, we gather near.

With lanterns aglow, we share every tale,
Of heroes and journeys that never grew stale.
In the heart of the woodlands, we stand hand in hand,
Together we revel in this enchanted land.

Glimmers Through the Frozen Boughs

Beneath a blanket of shimmering white,
Crystalized branches gleam in the light.
Glimmers of warmth in the cold winter's grasp,
Festive spirits release from their clasp.

Frosty whispers swirl through the trees,
Carried along by the brisk winter breeze.
Laughter dances brightly, silver and gold,
A tapestry woven, a story retold.

Candles aglow, their flickers align,
Illuminating smiles like stars that entwine.
In the hush of the evening, joy sparks anew,
As glimmers through boughs bring hope to pursue.

The world dressed in sparkle, a sight so divine,
We gather together, our hearts intertwine.
With every soft echo, we sing through the night,
Glimmers of love make the season so bright.

Tranquil Majesty of the Twilight Realm

In twilight's embrace, the day takes its bow,
Colors of magic weave soft shadows somehow.
Majesty dances on the edge of the dark,
Whispers of twilight igniting a spark.

Golden hues fade, giving way to the night,
Stars start to twinkle, their effortless light.
Under serene skies, laughter spills free,
In this tranquil realm, we're wild as the sea.

Gathering round, the warmth of the fire,
Stories unspoken stir hearts with desire.
Gentle and calm, as the night starts to swell,
Moments of bliss in the twilight's soft spell.

With each flickering flame, our spirits ignite,
Together we stand, bound in pure delight.
In tranquil majesty, we find our way,
As the twilight whispers, we welcome the day.

Enchanted by the Crystal Shroud

Wrapped in the shroud of a mystical light,
Enchantment surrounds us, twinkling so bright.
Every soft whisper, each glimmering seam,
Comes alive in the night, like a beautiful dream.

Crystals like stardust, adorn every branch,
Inviting our hearts in a magical dance.
Laughter entwines with the frosty air,
Together we journey, through realms beyond care.

Beneath the bright moon, we twirl and we spin,
In the splendor of moments where dreams can begin.
The night hums a tune, sweet as honeyed wine,
In a world steeped in joy, every heart becomes fine.

Enchanted we stand, embraced by the glow,
As the crystal shroud whispers secrets we know.
In this festive embrace, we lose track of time,
Caught in the magic, our spirits in rhyme.

Reverie of the Woodland Monarchs

Beneath the boughs, the whispers play,
Dancing leaves in bright array.
Soft sunlight filters through the trees,
Nature's laughter in the breeze.

Frolic some fae with wings so bright,
Their laughter fills the warm daylight.
Gathered crowns of petals fine,
Woodland joys, in love entwine.

Squirrels dart with nimble grace,
Curious eyes of wonder trace.
A symphony of life unfolds,
Tales of magic gently told.

In this realm where spirits gleam,
Every moment feels like a dream.
Woodland monarchs, reign you must,
In nature's heart, we place our trust.

Beneath the Glistening Canopy

Twinkling lights in every shade,
Glistening leaves, with joy displayed.
Amidst the branches, shadows weave,
Nature's wonder, we believe.

Birds chirp sweet in harmony,
Songs that soothe and set us free.
Beneath the canopy, we cheer,
Each vibrant heartbeat brings us near.

A banquet spread on mossy grounds,
With fragrant blooms and merry sounds.
Gather 'round to share the cheer,
In this haven, we hold dear.

Time stands still as spirits soar,
Magic lingers, evermore.
Beneath the glistening you will find,
A revelry of heart and mind.

The Ethereal World of Winter's Embrace

In winter's arms, a chill in air,
Whispers soft, a dream to share.
Blankets white on every ground,
In this silence, joy is found.

Snowflakes twirl like tiny sprites,
Dancing softly, pure delights.
Fires crackle, glow so bright,
Stories told of winter's night.

Joyful laughter fills the scene,
Friends and family, hearts serene.
Carols sung beneath the stars,
Warmth of love, despite the bars.

In every flake, a wish bestowed,
On this path, our hearts bestowed.
An ethereal world, we embrace,
Winter's beauty, a warm grace.

Emblazoned in Frozen Splendor

Amidst the frost, the colors gleam,
Nature woven in a dream.
Trees adorned with crystal lace,
A moment captured, time's embrace.

Icicles hang like chandeliers,
Reflecting sunlight, warming spheres.
Each step whispers on the ice,
In this beauty, pure and nice.

Children laugh and spirits soar,
Snowball fights and hearts explore.
Every glance, a treasure found,
In frozen splendor, we are bound.

Emblazoned hues in winter's hold,
A tapestry of joy unfolds.
With every breath, we sing and sway,
In nature's art, we find our way.

Flicker of Light in the Frosted Woods

In the woods where the snowflakes dance,
Candles flicker in a merry prance.
Whispers of joy in the crisp night air,
Soft shadows twinkle, a magical flair.

Tree branches wear coats of shimmering white,
Beneath the moon's glow, everything's bright.
Laughter erupts like a bubbling stream,
Frosted wonderland, bathed in a dream.

The scent of pine fills the chilly space,
As friends gather close, each smiling face.
Harmony sings through the chilly night,
In this charming scene, hearts feel so light.

Glimmers of hope in the winter's embrace,
Together we dance, in this joyful place.
Magic is real in the still of the night,
Flicker of joy in the frosted light.

Ballet of Shadows in the Icy Glen

In the glen where the icy winds play,
Shadows waltz in a glorious array.
Snowflakes swirl like a ballerina's twirl,
As the frosty night begins to unfurl.

Bright stars above in the velvet blue,
Glow down gently, as if on cue.
Rhythms of laughter echo and soar,
As friends come together, spirits to explore.

With every step in this winter's delight,
Joy leaps and bounds in the shimmering light.
Frosted whispers carry tales of the past,
In this balletic dance, the spell is cast.

Embracing the cold with warm, tender smiles,
Together we frolic through magical miles.
In the icy glen, our worries take flight,
Ballet of shadows in the blanket of night.

Echoes of Ancient Guardians in Winter's Shroud

In the hush of the night where the forests lie,
Echoes whisper beneath the vast sky.
Guardians of old, with a watchful grace,
Warmth in their hearts despite winter's face.

Frost blankets roots of the ancient trees,
The murmurs of spirits dance in the breeze.
Stories unfold in the shimmering glow,
As laughter resounds through the crisp, silent snow.

In the arms of the night, we gather near,
Filling the air with warmth and cheer.
Together we share in the warmth of the fire,
Content in this moment, our hearts lift higher.

With each passing hour, fond memories grow,
Echoes of joy in the soft fallen snow.
With ancient guardians, we step, hand in hand,
In winter's shroud, forever we stand.

In The Heart of Frosted Whispers

In the heart where the frosted whispers play,
Secrets of winter come out to sway.
Glistening ribbons of white intertwine,
With laughter and mirth swirling through the pine.

Fires crackle, warm glow in the night,
As stories unfold, capturing the light.
Voices like melodies fill the cool air,
In the heart of the night, we gather with care.

Snowflakes fall softly, a blanket of dreams,
Each twinkling star bursting at the seams.
Season of magic, of wonder and glee,
In the frost-kissed embrace, we are wild and free.

Joy blooms like flowers in winter's cold grip,
United in this festive, joyful trip.
In the heart of it all, we cherish the glow,
Frosted whispers remind us to grow.

Glimmering Hooves on Frozen Earth

In the hush of winter's night,
Glimmers dance with pure delight,
Hooves clatter on the frosted ground,
Magic lingers all around.

Stars above in twinkling arrays,
Light the path of joyful days,
Children's laughter fills the air,
As wonders weave, beyond compare.

The crisp air whispers songs of cheer,
While hearts beat strong with festive fear,
Glistening dreams in silver hues,
Wrap us tight in winter's muse.

Moments shared with warmth and love,
As if blessed from skies above,
Beneath this blanket, pure and bright,
We find our joy in snowy light.

The Frosted Parade

A parade of colors bright,
Marching forth in pure delight,
With rosy cheeks and laughter loud,
We dance beneath the snowy cloud.

Banners wave, all gleam and glow,
While cheerful songs in chorus flow,
The frost has dressed the world anew,
In shimmering white, a stunning view.

Candies shared and cocoa sipped,
As joyous hearts are gently gripped,
The festive air, it sings and spins,
Uniting all in myriad wins.

So let us cheer for all we see,
In this parade of unity,
With every step, our spirits rise,
In celebration, 'neath winter skies.

Secrets Beneath the Shimmer

Beneath the frost, secrets abide,
In the icy depths, dreams reside,
Whispers echo through the trees,
As snowflakes fall upon the breeze.

Glittering paths, a hidden lore,
Awaits in silence, evermore,
With every twinkle, tales unfold,
Of joys and wonders yet untold.

Ember fires crackle bright,
Warming hearts on this cold night,
As laughter spills in cozy homes,
While outside, frosted magic roams.

Let's gather 'round and share our dreams,
In light of hope, or so it seems,
For underneath each mushy snow,
Lies the warmth of love we show.

Chasing Frosted Dreams

Chasing dreams on frosted floors,
Through the night, the laughter soars,
A playground dressed in icy white,
We revel in this wintry sight.

Wrapped in scarves, we laugh and glide,
As joy and wonder swell inside,
With every spin, we chase the glee,
As magic swirls, we feel so free.

Crisp air sparks each breath with hope,
As we dance, our spirits cope,
The world transforms with every glance,
Inviting all to join the dance.

So let us leap, our hearts ablaze,
In these frosted, festive days,
With dreams aglow, we'll never tire,
For winter's chill fuels our fire.

www.ingramcontent.com/pod-product-compliance
Ingram Content Group UK Ltd.
Pitfield, Milton Keynes, MK11 3LW, UK
UKHW020104171224
452675UK00013B/1321